Who Was Alexander the Great?

Alexander the Great Biography for Kids

Tanya Turner

PUBLISHED BY:

Tanya Turner

Copyright © 2018

All rights reserved.

No part of this publication may be copied, reproduced in any format, by any means, electronic or otherwise, without prior consent from the copyright owner and publisher of this book.

Disclaimer

The information contained in this book is for general information purposes only. The information is provided by the authors and, while we endeavor to keep the information up to date and correct, we make no representations or warranties of any kind, expressed or implied, about the completeness, accuracy, reliability, suitability or availability with respect to the book or the information, products, services, or related graphics contained in the book for any purpose. Any reliance you place on such information is therefore strictly at your own risk.

TABLE OF CONTENTS

Alexander the Great Biography 7

Early Life 9

Education 10

Alexander's Destiny 11

King Philip II Marries Again 14

Death of King Philip II 16

King Alexander II's Consolidation of Power 17

Conquest of Persian Empire 19

Alexander and Hephaestion 21

Division of Empire 24

Alexander the Great Biography

Alexander the Great was one of the most famous kings of the ancient Greek kingdom of Macedon. Although he died young at only 32 years of age, he nevertheless conquered more kingdoms and empires than any of his predecessors.

His success can be attributed to his upbringing as he was trained both intellectually and militarily from a young age. There were also legends about him having divine parentage that made him destined for greatness.

King Alexander III of Macedon, also known as Alexander the Great

Photo courtesy of Wikimedia

Early Life

Alexander III of Macedon, or Alexander the Great, was born on July 20 or 21, 356 BC in Pella. His father was *King Philip II*.

His mother, *Olympias*, was King Philip II's 4th wife. Around the time that Alexander was born, she was considered to be his main wife.

There were some legends as to Alexander's birth, and it can't be said whether or not these were just made up by his mother. According to Olympias, the night before she became King Philip the II's wife, she dreamt that her womb was hit by a thunderbolt.

Philip III also had a dream not long after, wherein he was said to be putting a seal with a lion's image on Olympia's womb.

During Alexander's birth, the *Temple of Artemis* was burned down. The people attributed the mishap to Artemis' absence in the temple in order to attend Alexander's birth. Artemis is the Greek Goddess of the Hunt

At this time, King Philip III was on one of his military campaigns.

Education

King Philip II hired *Aristotle* to tutor his son, Alexander. Aristotle is one of the greatest philosophers of Ancient Time. The *Temple of the Nymphs* at Mieza became their classroom; and Aristotle took charge of teaching Alexander different subjects like philosophy, medicine, religion, art, logic, and more.

Some of Alexander's friends attended the same class taught by Aristotle. *Ptolemy*, *Cassander*, and *Hephaestion*, all companions of Alexander, were the future generals of his army.

Alexander's father, King Philip II, hired the best teachers to show his son how to play the lyre, ride a horse, and fight as a soldier. He was already grooming Alexander to be his successor.

Alexander's Destiny

Alexander showed courage and heroism even when he was a

Statue of Alexander the Great and his mother, Olympias

Photo courtesy of Wikimedia

young boy. There was a time when King Philip wanted to buy him a horse, but the horse was wild. His father considered not buying the horse, but Alexander was able to tame it.

Alexander named his horse Bucephalas and he rode it up to India during his conquests of kingdoms. It was said that Bucephalas died of old age (30 years old) and Alexander named a city after his horse.

When Alexander was 16 years old, King Philip II led a war against the Byzantion. He left Alexander in charge of the palace as his heir apparent to the throne.

When Thracian Maedi heard that King Philip II was away, they started a revolt against Macedonia. Alexander, however, was quick to act. He led the troops that his father left behind to drive the Thracians from their own territory. He then colonized Thracia and named one of its cities *Alexandropolis*.

When King Philip II returned from war, he and his son joined forces to attack other kingdoms and empires so they could expand their own.

King Philip II Marries Again

King Philip II married *Cleopatra Eurydice,* who was the niece of Attalus, one of the king's generals. During the wedding feast, Attalus prayed to the gods for a legitimate heir for King Philip II's throne. According to him, a son born from Philip II and Cleopatra would have pure Macedonian blood. Alexander was only half-Macedonian.

Attalus' speech angered Alexander and he stood up to rebuke Attalus. His father, King Philip II, went to Attalus' defense and acted to hurt Alexander. But since the king and the guests of the feasts were already drunk, he slipped.

Fearing for his life, Alexander left Macedon and went to Illyria. However, his father never really changed his mind about giving his throne to Alexander, and they reconciled. Alexander then went back to Macedonia after being away for six months.

Alexander was also known as the Conqueror of the Persian Empire
Photo courtesy of Wikipedia

Death of King Philip II

King Philip II and Olympia had a daughter named Cleopatra. When King Philip II attended the wedding feast of her daughter Cleopatra, *Pausanias* assassinated him. Pausanias was the captain of his bodyguards.

Pausanias then tried to escape those who were pursuing him, but he tripped on a vine and fell. He was killed right there.

Alexander was only 20 when his father died. He was proclaimed king by the nobles, and this decision was supported by the army.

King Alexander III's Consolidation of Power

Alexander wanted to make sure that he had no rivals for the throne, so he made it a point to get rid of all his potential threats. One of the first ones to be executed was his cousin *Amyntas VI*. He also had 2 Macedonian princes killed.

His mother, Olympias, had King Philip II's other wife Cleopatra and her children killed in order to secure the throne for her son Alexander.

Alexander wasn't aware of his mother's plans to have Cleopatra and her children killed, and this made him angry. The incident made him decide to have Attalus murdered.

Attalus was one of the commanders of the Macedonian army, and there were rumors that he was planning to defect to Athens after King Philip II's death. Aside from that, he was also Cleopatra's uncle; and Alexander thought that it could be risky if he were allowed to stay alive.

Ptolemy, one of Alexander the Great's generals

Photo courtesy of Wikipedia

Conquest of Persian Empire

Alexander the Great had many accomplishments as a military commander in Macedonia's army. In fact, he never lost a battle even when his troops were outnumbered by enemy troops. Aside from having loyal followers, Alexander himself was great at forming tactics, strategies, and counterattacks.

His greatest accomplishment, however, was the *conquest of the Persian Empire,* which was really strong and powerful at that time. After a series of victories, Persia surrendered to Alexander.

This was a great accomplishment, and Alexander was called the *Conqueror of the Persian Empire.* This, however, led to some problems as his Macedonian subjects and Persian subjects couldn't get along with one another.

Alexander and Hephaestion

Hephaestion was Alexander's childhood friend, and they remained close friends even through adulthood. In fact, he was the second-in-command in Alexander's army. There were even some reports that he could have been Alexander's lover.

Hephaestion died unexpectedly when he fell ill, and this devastated Alexander. The cause of death can't be established, but it's possible that he was poisoned. Nevertheless, it was said that Alexander became angry at Hephaestion's doctor when he was unable to cure him, so he had him executed.

Alexander declared a public mourning for his friend and he

even ordered funeral rites fit for a king. Alexander grieved for Hephaestion for a really long time.

Alexander (left) and his friend and bodyguard, Hephaestion (right)
Photo courtesy of Wikipedia.

Death

Alexander's death was a controversial one and it's still considered a mystery to this day. On one account, it is said that Alexander developed a fever after drinking a lot of wine. The fever eventually paralyzed him, and he died in less than 2 weeks.

Another account says that Alexander felt pain after gulping down a cup of wine. The pain was great and it made him weak, but he did not develop a fever. Alexander is said to have died in pain.

Today, foul play and poisoning are considered to be possible causes of Alexander's death. *Antipater* is considered a suspect as he was at odds with Olympias. And having been summoned to Babylon, he was anticipating that he would be killed. Since his son, Iollas, was Alexander's wine pourer, it was quite possible that he poisoned the king. There were even suggestions of Aristotle's participation in this event.

Natural causes were and are still being considered, too. Diseases like malaria and typhoid fever can have the same symptoms that Alexander experienced before he died.

His failing health due to excessive drinking and severe wounds during battle could have also caused complications. Hephaestion's death may have contributed to his weakening condition as well.

Alexander the Great died on June 10 or 11, 323 BC at the age of 32.

Division of Empire

After Alexander III's death, his empire was divided into 4.

Although witnesses saw Alexander gave his signet ring to *Perdiccas* as a sign that he was nominating him as the next king, he didn't become king. Instead, he was assassinated.

Alexander's 4 generals, *Ptolemy*, *Cassander*, *Seleucus*,and *Antigous,* became rivals as they tried to take over Alexander's empire. The division of the empire continued up to their heirs. This eventually led to the fall of the Macedonian empire as none of the 4 kings who took over after Alexander were able to unite the kingdoms again.

Made in the USA
Coppell, TX
15 June 2021